Passing The PRINCE® 2
Examinations

CCTA
Central Computer and Telecommunications Agency

LONDON: The Stationery Office

First published 1999

ISBN 0 11 330013 1

For further information regarding this and other CCTA products please contact:
CCTA Library
Rosebery Court
St Andrews Business Park
Norwich NR7 0HS
Telephone: 01603 704567

Published by The Stationery Office and available from:

The Publications Centre
(mail, telephone and fax orders only)
PO Box 276, London SW8 5DT
General enquiries 0171 873 0011
Telephone orders 0171 873 9090
Fax orders 0171 873 8200

The Stationery Office Bookshops
123 Kingsway, London WC2B 6PQ
0171 242 6393 Fax 0171 242 6394
68–69 Bull Street, Birmingham B4 6AD
0121 236 9696 Fax 0121 236 9699
33 Wine Street, Bristol BS1 2BQ
0117 926 4306 Fax 0117 929 4515
9–21 Princess Street, Manchester M60 8AS
0161 834 7201 Fax 0161 833 0634
16 Arthur Street, Belfast BT1 4GD
01232 238451 Fax 01232 235401
The Stationery Office Oriel Bookshop
18–19 High Street, Cardiff CF1 2BZ
01222 395548 Fax 01222 384347
71 Lothian Road, Edinburgh EH3 9AZ
0131 228 4181 Fax 0131 622 7017

The Stationery Office's Accredited Agents
(see Yellow Pages)

and through good booksellers

Printed in the UK for The Stationery Office
J74167 3/99 9385 9988

Contents

Foreword

This book is aimed at easing the path for all those intending to take the CCTA/APM Group PRINCE 2 Foundation and Practitioner examinations.

Thanks go to Colin Bentley for checking the content and adding the invaluable "Checklist" for the Practitioner examination and to Dave Purves for his helpful input. Also to the APM Group and the PRINCE 2 Examination Board for allowing the use of PRINCE 2 examination material, and Richard Pharro for general support and assistance in getting this publication to print.

I hope you will find this book of real use in preparing for, and passing, your examination.

If you have any views or comments on this book, please forward them to CCTA.

CCTA
Best Practice Customer Service Desk
Rosebery Court
St Andrews Business Park
Norwich
NR7 0HS

Ken Bradley

March 1999

Passing The PRINCE 2 Examinations – The Foundation Exam

The Examination

The Foundation Examination is a one-hour, closed book exam. The examination is designed to test the Candidate's knowledge of the PRINCE 2 Method by choosing the correct answer from a selection of possible answers. There are 75 Questions in all and Candidates must score 38 correct answers or more to pass. There is no consolidation or carry-forward of time or scores to the Practitioner Examination - the exam stands alone. Candidates intending to take the PRINCE 2 Practitioner Examination (or any other PRINCE-related exam) must first pass the Foundation Exam.

The Track Record

Statistics released by the APM Group to PRINCE 2 Accredited Training Organisations (ATOs) show that just under 95% of all Candidates can expect to pass the Foundation Exam indicating that the level of understanding of the PRINCE 2 Method, usually achieved following an accredited training event, is high.

Only around 65% of Candidates taking the Practitioner Exam succeeded, indicating that the Candidates' ability to take a project scenario and answer questions with reference to the PRINCE 2 Method, thereby demonstrating they are able to apply the Method to a practical situation, is comparatively low. A later section of this publication provides advice and guidance on the Practitioner Exam.

The Foundation Examination

On the following pages are examples of the questions and multiple choice answers that make up the Foundation Exam. Do not approach the questions "cold"; you must have done quite a bit of preparation before attempting any of the exam questions otherwise you will get demoralised!

There are around 250 questions in the APM Group database from which the actual examination questions are taken. Some of the questions are very straightforward and will give you little trouble; others drill down into the Method and are there to really test your knowledge. You will find that some of the possible answers posed can be eliminated with even a basic knowledge of the Method.

Preparing for The Exam

Success in the Foundation Exam requires a good understanding of what makes up the PRINCE 2 Method and the flows of information within it. As part of your preparation for the exam, it is well worth producing an overall detailed Process Map of PRINCE 2 from the Process Method and context diagrams given in the official Stationery Office PRINCE 2 Manual (Managing Successful Projects with PRINCE 2 - ISBN 0 11 330855 8).

The approach is to take each of the major Processes (excluding "Planning") and map the flows of information and Products between them to produce a diagram similar to the following:

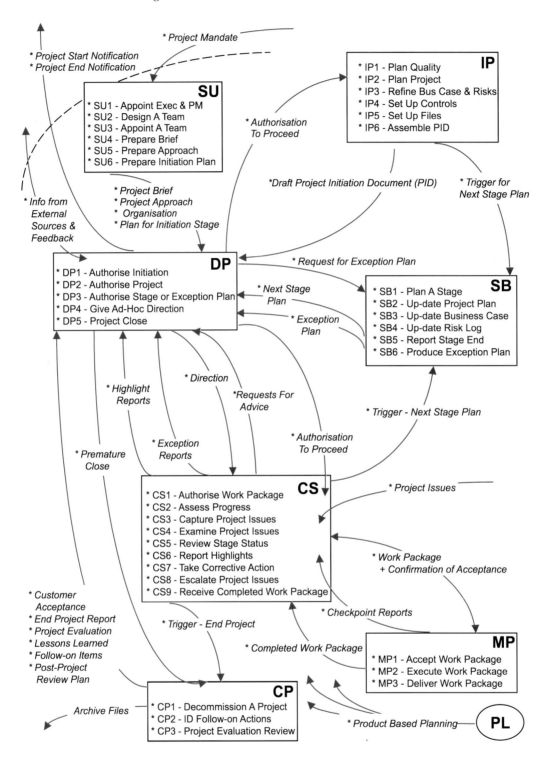

The Planning Process may be treated as a "backdrop" to the other seven major Processes, providing the required planning input as required.

To get the most out of this exercise, a break-down of each major Process into its Processes is recommended to show the specific "to and from" relationships between the Processes. If you do this, your final Process Map will be considerably more detailed than the one shown above; you must produce your own diagram - do not rely on the one shown!

Remember that the main benefit from creating your summary Process Map will come from the research you will need to do into each Process. You will not be allowed to take your Summary Process Map into the Foundation Examination but it will be a useful revision aid and helpful in structuring the content of the Practitioner Examination answers.

Technique for Completing The Foundation Examination

The best technique for the Foundation Exam is to go through the paper in an initial non-stop "sweep", answering all the straightforward questions which you know the answers to; ignore any long, wordy questions or those which might need some working out (ie double-negative questions). The examiners are fond of including "negative" questions (ie *"which of the following is NOT ...."*) and you might find it easier to return to these at a later time.

When your first sweep is completed you should have most of the questions answered; typically this will take about 25-35 minutes. You can, at this stage, count up the number of questions you know you have answered correctly to provide a confidence boost - but be sure this will not have the opposite effect!

Now return to those more obscure or difficult questions. Many will not be as tricky as they first appeared and with a bit of common-sense and eradication of the obvious non-starter answers you should be able to pick up most of the marks.

Beware of changing answers you already have - experience indicates that about two thirds of changes made to the Foundation Exam answers are changes from correct to incorrect. If you need to make a change show it clearly.

You should now be ready for a go at a trial Foundation Examination paper - if you have done your preparation work you should be feeling pretty confident and ready to tackle the example exam which starts on the next page. Always plan your approach to the real exam - time the completion of the example paper that follows for no more than two days before the examination - you will then be finely honed - with just enough time to review the elements you missed out on but not too much time to cause you to lose the cutting edge you'll need for the real thing.

Good luck!

The Professional Examinations

Date . . . .

Foundation Examination Paper

Multiple Choice

Instructions

1   All 75 Questions should be attempted

2.   There are no trick questions

3.   All answers are to be marked on the original examination paper

4.   Please use a pen to mark your answers with either a ✓ or X. There is only one correct answer per question unless more than one is specified for that question

5.   You have 1 hour for this paper

6.   You must get 50% (38 or more Questions) correct to pass

Candidate Number: ....

1:   Which of the following is NOT a PRINCE 2 Component?

   a)   Configuration Management   ☐
   b)   Stages   ☐
   c)   Work Package   ☑
   d)   Organisation   ☐
   e)   Planning   ☐

2:   The majority of PRINCE 2 controls are described as:

   a)   Technique-based   ☐
   b)   Component-driven   ☐
   c)   Project Manager-driven   ☐
   d)   Ad-hoc   ☐
   e)   Event-based   ☑

3:   In terms of a Product Breakdown Structure, what type of Product is the Issue Log?

   a)   A Specialist Product   ☐
   b)   A Management Product   ☐
   c)   A Quality Product   ☑
   d)   A Technical Product   ☐
   e)   None of these   ☐

4:   What role should check that a Product is ready for a Quality Review?

   a)   The Chairman   *MEANING THE QUALITY CHAIRMAN*   ☐   *A*
   b)   The Producer   ☐
   c)   The Project Manager   ☐
   d)   The Reviewers   ☐
   e)   The QR Secretary   ☑

5:   Who should ensure that Tolerance is set for the Project?

   a)   The Executive   ☑
   b)   The Project Board   ☐
   c)   The Senior User   ☐
   d)   The Project Manager   ☐

6:   Does PRINCE 2 recommend a minimum number of Stages? - if so what is the recommendation?

   a)   One   ☐
   b)   Two   ☑
   c)   Three   ☐
   d)   It makes no difference   ☐
   e)   No minimum is recommended   ☐

7:   What name is given to an Off-Specification which is accepted by the Project Board without corrective action?

   a)   Exception Report   ☐
   b)   Exception Memo   ☐
   c)   Change Contingency   ☐
   d)   Concession   ☑
   e)   Project Issue   ☐

8:   When does a Team Manager report on the status of a Work Package to the
     Project Manager?

    a)   Weekly   ☐
    b)   Daily   ☐
    c)   At the frequency defined in the Work Package   ☑
    d)   Ad-hoc   ☐

9:   What comes first in PRINCE 2?

    a)   Project Brief   ☐
    b)   Feasibility Study   ☐
    c)   Scoping Study   ☐
    d)   Acceptance Criteria   ☐
    e)   Customer's Quality Expectations   ☐
    f)   Project Mandate   ☑

10: Who is appointed in the first Process (Starting Up A Project (SU1))?

    a)   The Project Board Executive   ☐
    b)   The Project Manager   ☐
    c)   Both the above   ☑
    d)   The Project Board   ☐
    e)   The Project Management Team   ☐

11: Which of these Processes does NOT trigger the Planning (PL) Process?

    a)   Controlling A Stage (CS)   ☑
    b)   Starting Up A Project (SU)   ☐
    c)   Managing Stage Boundaries (SB)   ☐
    d)   Initiating A Project (IP)   ☐

12: Which of these is NOT a specific objective of an End Stage Assessment?

    a)   Check that the need for the project is unchanged   ☐
    b)   Review the next stage plan against the project plan   ☐
    c)   Disseminate useful lessons learned   ☑
    d)   Review the Tolerances set for the next Stage   ☐

13: Does PRINCE 2 cover …

    a)   The Product Lifecycle   ☐
    b)   The Project Lifecycle   ☐
    c)   The Project Lifecycle plus some pre-project preparation   ☑
    d)   The Project Lifecycle plus some post-project Activity   ☐
    e)   The complete Project and Product Lifecycle   ☐

14: What provision can be made in Planning for implementing Requests For
     dealing with expected Change?

    a)   Project & Stage Tolerances   ☐
    b)   A Change Budget   ☑
    c)   Contingency Plans   ☐
    d)   Adding Contingency to estimates   ☐

15: In the Planning Process, which Process comes before "Estimating"?

    a)   Identifying Activities & Dependencies   ☑
    b)   Analysing Risks   ☐
    c)   Completing A Plan   ☐
    d)   Scheduling   ☐
    e)   Defining & Analysing Products   ☐

16: What action should a Reviewer take on finding a grammatical mistake in a Product under review?

    a)   Note it on an Error List   ☐
    b)   Advise the Producer   ☐
    c)   Note it on the Follow-Up Action List   ☐
    d)   Annotate the Product copy   ☑
    e)   Advise the Quality Review Scribe   ☐

17: Which of these statements is FALSE?

    a)   A PRINCE 2 project has a finite life span   ☐
    b)   A PRINCE 2 project has a defined amount of Resources   ☐
    c)   A PRINCE 2 project has an organisation structure with defined responsibilities to manage the project   ☐
    d)   A PRINCE 2 project may well have only activities with no associated Products   ☑

18: Which of these is NOT a Project Issue?

    a)   An Exception Report   ☑
    b)   A Request For Change   ☐
    c)   A Specialist Query   ☐
    d)   A Statement of Concern   ☐
    e)   All the above   ☐

19: Who is responsible for the "Managing Product Delivery (MP)" Process?

    a)   The Project Manager   ☐
    b)   The Senior Supplier   ☐
    c)   The Stage Manager   ☐
    d)   The Team Manager   ☑

20: Which Stage does PRINCE 2 recommend should always be used?

    a)   Implementation   ☐
    b)   Testing   ☐
    c)   Start-up   ☐
    d)   Initiation   ☑
    e)   Handover   ☐

21: Identify the two possible allowances which may have to be included within the project's plan structure

    a)   A Change Budget & Contingency Plans   ☑
    b)   Plan Levels & Planning Tools   ☐
    c)   Impact Analysis & Concessions   ☐
    d)   Mid Stage Assessments & Exception Reporting   ☐

22: What is created first in Product-Based Planning?

    a)   A Product Checklist   ☐
    b)   Product Descriptions   ☐
    c)   A Product Flow Diagram   ☐
    d)   Product Outlines   ☐
    e)   A Product Breakdown Structure   ☑

23: "Controlling A Stage (CS)" Drives which other Process?

    a)   Ad-Hoc Direction   ☐
    b)   Planning   ☐
    c)   Managing Stage Boundaries   ☐
    d)   Managing Product Delivery   ☑
    e)   Closing A Project   ☐

24: Which individual role is ultimately responsible for the project?

    a)   Senior User   ☐
    b)   Senior Supplier   ☐
    c)   Executive   ☑
    d)   Project Manager   ☐
    e)   Programme Director   ☐

25: In which Process is the Project Management Team reviewed for changes?

    a)   Planning A Stage   ☑
    b)   Reporting Stage End   ☐
    c)   Updating A Project Plan   ☐
    d)   Reviewing Stage Status   ☐

26: What is a direct input to the Project Quality Plan?

    a)   ISO9001 QMS   ☐
    b)   The Corporate Quality Policy   ☐
    c)   The Business Case   ☐
    d)   Quality Reviewers' Assignments   ☐
    e)   Customer Quality Expectations   ☑

27: What does PRINCE 2 regard as the driving force of the project?

    a)   The Risk Assessment (& Risk Log)   ☐
    b)   The Project Initiation Document   ☐
    c)   The Project Brief   ☐
    d)   The Business Benefits   ☑
    e)   The Customer's Project Mandate   ☐

28: Project Controls are set up based on the Project Brief, The Project Quality Plan, and ...

    a)   The Project Plan   ☐
    b)   The Risk Log   ☐
    c)   The Business Case   ☐
    d)   The Project Approach   ☑
    e)   The Project Mandate   ☐

29: Name the Product which measures the achievement of the Project's Benefits

    a)   End Project Notification   ☐
    b)   Lessons Learned Report   ☐
    c)   End Project Report   ☐
    d)   Post Project Review   ☑
    e)   Benefits Review Statement   ☐

30: In which Process is the Stage Plan updated with "actuals"?

    a)   Assessing Progress   ☑
    b)   Reviewing Stage Status   ☐
    c)   Planning A Stage   ☐
    d)   Reporting Highlights   ☐

31: When do the steps of "Directing A Project" begin

    a) Before "Starting Up A Project" ☐
    b) At Initiation of the project ☐
    c) During "Starting Up A Project" ☐
    d) After "Starting Up A Project" ☑
    e) From the receipt of the Project Mandate ☐

32: What does PRINCE 2 regard as the third project interest, given User and Supplier as the other two?

    a) Technical ☐
    b) Management ☐
    c) Business ☑
    d) Quality ☐
    e) Sponsor/Customer ☐

33: Which two steps are NOT part of "Accepting A Work Package" (Tick 2 Boxes)

    a) Understand the reporting requirements ☐
    b) Agree Tolerance Margins for the Product ☐
    c) Monitor and Control the Risks associated with the Work Package ☑
    d) Producing Checkpoint Reports ☑

34: Which statement is incorrect? Stages are ...

    a) The amount of work defined in a Work Package ☑
    b) Partitions of the Project with decision points ☐
    c) Collections of Activities and Products whose delivery is managed as a unit ☐
    d) A sub-set of the project ☐
    e) The element of work which the Project Manager is managing on behalf of the Project Board at any one time ☐

35: When should Reviewers be appointed for Quality Review?

    a) Project planning time ☐
    b) Stage planning time ☑
    c) Quality Review planning time ☐
    d) As early as possible in the project ☐

36: What time-driven control ascertains the status of Stage or Team work?

    a) Highlight Report ☐
    b) Checkpoint Report ☑
    c) End Stage Report ☐
    d) Exception Report ☐
    e) Product Review Status Report ☐
    f) Quality Review Sign-off ☐

37: Which one of these forms part of a PRINCE 2 plan?

    a) The Project Organisation ☐
    b) The Issues Log ☐
    c) Error Lists ☐
    d) The Risk Log ☐
    e) Points at which progress will be monitored and controlled ☑

38: What purpose does Risk Evaluation serve?

    a)   Decides whether the level of risk is acceptable   ☑

    b)   Determines how important each risk is   ☐

    c)   Determines potential risks to be faced   ☐

    d)   Assesses the consequences of each risk   ☐

39: The configuration of the final deliverable of the project is:-

    a)   The final Product itself   ☐

    b)   The interim Products   ☐

    c)   Its Product Description   ☐

    d)   The sum total of its Products   ☑

40: In which Process is the Project Brief formalised?

    a)   Starting Up A Project (SU)   ☑

    b)   Initiating A Project (IP)   ☐

    c)   Authorising Initiation (DP1)   ☐

    d)   Authorising A Project (DP2)   ☐

    e)   In the Project Mandate   ☐

41: Which phrase applies to the user representative(s) in a PRINCE 2 Project Management Team?

    a)   They will be impacted by the outcome   ☑

    b)   They may need to use in-house and/or external teams to construct the final outcome   ☐

    c)   They provide the Business viewpoint   ☐

    d)   They will provide the funding for the project   ☐

    e)   They are responsible for the final outcome   ☐

42: What other control is closely linked with Configuration Management?

    a)   Control of risk   ☐

    b)   Project Closure   ☐

    c)   Quality Review   ☐

    d)   Project Initiation   ☐

    e)   Change Control   ☑

43: When are the planned start and end dates added to the Product Checklist?

    a)   Scheduling   ☐

    b)   Completing A Plan   ☑

    c)   Analysing Risks   ☐

    d)   After "Authorising A Project (DP2)"   ☐

    e)   Updating A Project Plan   ☐

44: Who should re-evaluate the priority of a Project Issue after impact analysis?

    a)   The Project Manager   ☐

    b)   Those with Project Assurance responsibilities   ☐

    c)   The Senior user   ☑

    d)   The Executive Member   ☐

    e)   The Author/Originator   ☐

45: What is the input to the Process "Authorising A Project"?

    a)   The Project Brief   ☐

    b)   The Project Plan   ☐

    c)   A Draft Project Initiation Document   ☑

    d)   The Project's Business Case   ☐

46: In the Process "Updating A Project Plan" which other Products are possibly revised?

    a) The Risk Log and Business Case ☑
    b) The Project Quality Plan and Project Approach ☐
    c) The Project Management Team and Project Brief ☐
    d) The Lessons Learned Report and End Stage Report ☐
    e) The Project Mandate, Project Brief and PID ☐

47: Which role does PRINCE 2 suggest should canvas the Project Board for agreement to implement a Project Issue

    a) Senior User ☑
    b) Senior Supplier ☐
    c) Executive ☐
    d) Project Manager ☐
    e) Team Manager ☐

48: Which of the following is NOT a PRINCE 2 definition of a project?

    a) Has a finite and defined life span ☐
    b) Produces defined and measurable business products ☐
    c) Uses a defined amount of resources ☐
    d) Has an organisation structure ☐
    e) Uses a defined set of techniques ☑

49: Which of these is NOT a valid Risk Management action?

    a) Prevention ☐
    b) Reduction ☐
    c) Denial ☑
    d) Transference ☐
    e) Contingency ☐

50: Which of the following is NOT included in the Composition list of the Project Initiation Document Outline Product Description?

    a) Project Mandate ☑
    b) Initial Business Case ☐
    c) Project Quality Plan ☐
    d) Contingency Plan ☐

51: In which Process are Checkpoint Reports created?

    a) Assessing Progress ☐
    b) Reporting Highlights ☐
    c) Reviewing Stage Status ☐
    d) Executing A Work Package ☑

52: The three major types of file recommended in PRINCE 2 are the Management File, the Quality File and ...

    a) The Technical File ☐
    b) The Specialist File ☑
    c) The System File ☐
    d) The Products File ☐

53: In which Process is an Exception Report created?

    a) Reporting Highlights   ☐
    b) Escalating Project Issues   ☑
    c) Taking Corrective Action   ☐
    d) Reviewing Stage Status   ☐
    e) Assessing Progress   ☐

54: In which Process should the Customer's Quality Expectations first be understood?

    a) Starting Up A Project   ☑
    b) Initiating A Project   ☐
    c) Authorising A Project   ☐
    d) Authorising Initiation   ☐

55: Risk Analysis comprises Risk Identification, Risk Estimation and ...

    a) Risk Actions   ☐
    b) Risk Reduction   ☐
    c) Risk Evaluation   ☑
    d) Risk Planning   ☐

56: What lists the major Products to be produced, with their key delivery dates?

    a) Product Breakdown Structure   ☐
    b) Product Description   ☐
    c) Product Flow Diagram   ☐
    d) Product Checklist   ☑

57: Which function creates, maintains and monitors the use of a Quality System?

    a) Quality Assurance   ☐
    b) Project Support   ☐   A
    c) The Project Assurance Team   ☑
    d) The Project Board   ☐

58: On completion of a Work Package, assessment of the work performed may contribute to what?

    a) Highlight Reporting   ☐
    b) Checkpoint Reporting   ☐
    c) Performance Appraisal   ☑
    d) Assessing Progress   ☐

59: Refining the Business Case and Risk Log up-dates ...

    a) The Project Plan   ☐
    b) The Issues Log   ☐   A
    c) The Project Initiation Document   ☑
    d) The Project Brief   ☐

60: Risk Management consists of Planning, Monitoring, Controlling and ...

    a) Estimation   ☐
    b) Assessment   ☐   D
    c) Execution   ☑
    d) Resourcing   ☐

61: Quality Management is ensuring that

    a)   A Quality Management System is created   ☐

    b)   The Customer's Quality Expectations are met   ☑

    c)   Quality Requirements are met   ☐

    d)   Product Quality Criteria are set   ☐

62: What is the name of the job a Team Manager carries out for the Project Manager?

    a)   A Team Plan   ☐

    b)   A Product Description   ☐

    c)   A Work Package   ☑

    d)   Resolving A Project Issue   ☐

63: In which file is the Risk Log kept?

    a)   The Project File   ☐

    b)   The Specialist File   ☐

    c)   The System File   ☐

    d)   The Products File   ☐

    e)   The Stage File   ☐

    f)   The Quality File   ☑

64: In the Process "Decommissioning A Project" the files are archived - what is the reason for this?

    a)   To provide useful lessons learned   ☐

    b)   To permit future audit   ☑

    c)   Never throw anything away   ☐

    d)   To provide management information   ☐

65: A list of the major Products to be produced is a component of ...

    a)   Configuration Management   ☐

    b)   A Product Description   ☐

    c)   A Plan   ☑

    d)   The Project Mandate   ☐

66: What are described as the "Assets" of a project?

    a)   Its Business Benefits   ☐

    b)   Its Resources   ☐

    c)   The Products   ☑

    d)   The Plans   ☐

    e)   The Project Management Team   ☐

67: The Project Plan is based on the Project Brief, the Project Quality Plan and which other Product?

    a)   The Project Approach   ☑

    b)   The Business Case   ☐

    c)   The Issue Log   ☐

    d)   The Risk Log   ☐

    e)   The Project Initiation Document   ☐

68: Apart from the Issue Log, what else is up-dated by the Process "Examining Project issues"?

    a)   Lessons Learned   ☐
    b)   Business Case   ☐
    c)   Risk Log   ☐
    d)   Stage Plan   ☑

C

69: Which of these is NOT an input to "Producing An Exception Plan (SB6)"?

    a)   Current Stage Plan   ☐
    b)   Exception Report   ☐
    c)   Lessons Learned Report   ☑
    d)   Issues Log   ☐

70: Which activity in Risk Analysis determines how important each identified risk is?

    a)   Risk Estimation   ☑
    b)   Risk Evaluation   ☐
    c)   Risk Measurement   ☐
    d)   Risk Management   ☐
    e)   Risk Planning   ☐

71: Which Product is not created within the PRINCE 2 Process Model?

    a)   The Project plan   ☐
    b)   The Project Mandate   ☑
    c)   The Project Brief   ☐
    d)   The Business Case   ☐
    e)   The Project Initiation Document   ☐

72: In which top-level Process are the files for the project created?

    a)   Starting Up A Project   ☐
    b)   Initiating A Project   ☑
    c)   Controlling A Stage   ☐
    d)   Managing Product Delivery   ☐

73: In the Customer:Supplier environment, which role is NOT included on the Supplier Project Board?

    a)   Senior Supplier   ☐
    b)   Supplier Skills Management   ☐
    c)   Customer Account Manager   ☐
    d)   Executive   ☑

74: In Programme Management, which role is likely to be the author of the final Business Case for funding Programme Work?

    a)   Programme Director   ☐
    b)   Programme Manager   ☐
    c)   Programme Executive - Change Authority   ☑
    d)   Change Manager   ☐

D

75: Which of the following is NOT a Quality Product?

    a)   Issue Log   ☐
    b)   Risk Log   ☑
    c)   Product Description   ☐
    d)   Quality Review Documentation   ☐

Now check your answers against the marking grid below and record your score.

Total Score: | 65 |

Marking Your Paper

Now you have completed the example Foundation Exam Paper, check your answers against those shown in the following table and look up the page number references for any questions you answered incorrectly. You should, realistically, be looking for a score of between 60-65 correct answers and completion within 40-50 minutes. Remember, for the actual examination you need to score 38 correct answers in 60 minutes.

Question	Answer	Question	Answer	Question	Answer
1	C	26	E	51	D
2	E	27	D	52	B
3	C	28	B	53	B
4	A	29	D	54	A
5	A	30	A	55	C
6	B	31	D	56	D
7	D	32	C	57	A
8	C	33	C & D	58	C
9	F	34	A	59	A
10	C	35	B	60	D
11	A	36	B	61	B
12	C	37	E	62	C
13	C	38	A	63	A
14	B	39	D	64	B
15	A	40	A	65	C
16	D	41	A	66	C
17	D	42	E	67	A
18	A	43	B	68	C
19	D	44	C	69	C
20	D	45	C	70	A
21	A	46	B	71	B
22	E	47	A	72	B
23	D	48	E	73	D
24	C	49	C	74	D
25	A	50	A	75	B

Passing The PRINCE 2 Examinations – The Practitioner Exam

The Practitioner Examination

You must first have passed the PRINCE 2 Foundation Examination in order to sit the Practitioner Exam. The PRINCE 2 Practitioner Examination is a 3 hour, open book exam. You may take the PRINCE 2 Manual and any notes into the exam. A Computer or any other electronic reference material is not allowed. The examination is designed to test your ability to apply the principles of the Method to a given scenario, by answering specific questions. There is a short scenario and three questions similar to the following:

PRINCE 2 Professional Examinations

The Practitioner Examination - Scenario
3 Hours Open-Book

Question 1: *How would you advise your colleague to tackle her organisation's quality expectations using the approaches in PRINCE 2?*

Question 2: *Produce a Product Breakdown Structure, Product Flow Diagram and a Product Description for any of the Products you have identified.*

Question 3: *Explain how the PRINCE 2 concept of Stages will help to control the project. Draw a diagram showing how and where the Stages might occur on your colleague's project.*

You have a colleague who is an experienced manager and administrator, but she is new to project management.

She has been assigned to manage the creation, publication and initial distribution of the company's next Annual Mail Order Catalogue. The Catalogue is aimed at the top end of a traditionally very demanding market and her management is concerned about building in quality as last year's publication went out late and with a number of errors.

The Company has been established for over 15 years and has migrated from an initial single retail outlet to over 70% of its turn-over (in excess of £50M per annum) arising from mail order. The Company Strategy is to continue to grow the mail order business as the net profit from this area of operation is up to 60% more than from sales of similar products through its 22 retail outlets.

The Catalogue will, as before, contain text and photographs printed on premium glossy paper. A photographic studio will be employed to provide up to 500 finished photographs of the company's products. The company's staff have been dealing with the same studio for the past 8 years and has built up a good relationship with the professional staff, although there is a feeling that the relationship is losing its business edge; a number of what is generally thought to be poor quality photos had to be included in last year's Catalogue as there was no time to re-shoot.

It is intended to place the text (describing the photographed products) with a professional copy-writing company. In the past this has been produced internally but there is a feeling that past efforts have been rather amateurish and lacking in "customer appeal". The decision to out-source this major and vital part of the Catalogue has come directly from the Managing Director and she has a lot riding on the outcome. The copy-writing company has just won a similar contract from a major competitor of your colleague's company and there is some disquiet about security and where loyalties might lie.

The company have no printing capability and will, as in the past, arrange for printing and distribution to be handled by an outside, independent, company. The printing company has offered to arrange distribution through a sub-contract, and has also offered to co-ordinate all Catalogue production aspects as they have good, long-term, relationships with the photographic studio and copy-writing company, as well as other sources in these fields. No decision has yet been made on this proposal.

Organisation:

Your colleague normally reports to a senior manager who in turn reports to a Board-level Director. For this project, she has been told she will report directly to the Managing Director.

The prime customer for the Catalogue is essentially the Sales Department, although many other Departments have a vested interest in its content. Examples of these other interested parties are the Technical Production Department and the Support Group who are anxious to ensure that accurate specifications are incorporated into the catalogue.

Your colleague has been advised that she can expect to have some administrative support (2-3 days per week) from a junior manager who has been with the company for about eight months. A part-time Sales Executive (maximum availability 1 day per week), and two nominees from the technical Departments (each available for not more than 2 days per week) complete the team. It is accepted that other resources from within the company will be used but only through the nominated team members.

There are about four months available for this project to be brought to completion and your colleague is obviously anxious to deliver a suitable end-product but is worried about the amount of work she will be expected to do herself as she has no specialist experience of the printing world.

A lot is riding on this project for all levels of management within the company. The market is very competitive and customers can be lost easily to some vigorous newcomers.

The preferred answer style is the use of "bullet" points, followed by up to three sentences (no more!) to show the examiner that you understand the *purpose, when it happens, who does it* and, where appropriate, the *content*; do not hide these vital, mark-scoring, points within an essay!

The marks available for each answer are divided between relatively few marks for the correct *identification* of an expected topic, plus an additional set of bonus marks for correctly *answering* the specific question, *explaining* the topic, *referring* to the PRINCE 2 Method, and *relating* it to the Scenario in the question paper. All answers must use the *correct PRINCE 2 Terminology* - generic responses will not attract good marks.

An example of how marks are distributed between relevant topics is shown overleaf. The table gives a good illustration of how the examiner's marking scheme is structured and the way the marks are allocated. The APM Group have issued an example Question Paper and Marking Scheme to the Accredited Training Organisations and this has been included at Appendix 1. The examiner will apportion marks generally on a one third/two thirds basis as indicated on the chart. Marks will be awarded for correctly identifying the relevant PRINCE 2 topics and further marks will be awarded for describing the relevance and usage of the topic as related to the specific question in the context of the given scenario.

TOPIC (Looked For By The Examiner)	Identify	Explain & Relate
Quality Expectations in Project Brief (+ Project Mandate)	1	–
Planning Quality, Quality Plan (IP1); Responsibilities; QMS	1	3
Work Package Authorisation + Agreement Proj Mgr/Team Mgr	2	2
Product Descriptions; Quality Criteria	2	3

Basically what's needed is to **Reference** the appropriate PRINCE 2 element, and then **Explain** and **Relate** its Nature, Relevance and Importance to the question posed - this advice should be heeded as it comes straight from the APM Group Examiners!

The Checklist

A straightforward checklist to help focus you on the Practitioner Examination paper has been made available to APM Group Accredited Training Organisations and it is reproduced below. Use it to guide you in preparing for and answering the paper.

- Don't write an essay. Start the answer with bullet points which list the names of those elements of PRINCE 2 that address the problem defined in the question. (Don't include PRINCE 2 areas that do not have a bearing on the question.) The only preamble should be one sentence that states, for example, "The PRINCE 2 elements that address this problem are:"

- Expand each bullet point with no more than two or three sentences that show that you understand:
  - What it is
  - When it is introduced into the project lifecycle
  - The purpose it serves
  - By whom it is used
  - How it works.

- Don't waste time "setting the scene" or reminding the examiner of what the question was.

- Don't refer the examiner to the manual for "a fuller explanation"

- Don't make assumptions that the examiner knows that you know anything about the PRINCE 2 Method.

- By all means explain (one sentence) any assumptions you are making about the scenario. Do not make any assumptions about the prior use of any part of PRINCE 2 in the project unless these are stated in the scenario.

- If it isn't in the scenario, don't introduce it. For example, if a question asks you to identify members of the project management team, don't identify people who are not in the scenario to take roles.

- Don't waffle. If a sentence is not making a specific point about a PRINCE 2 element that contributes to the answer, don't write it.

- Answer the question. No marks are awarded for mentioning a PRINCE 2 element which does not apply to the question, e.g. if the question is about quality, **don't** mention that the Project Board review the business case at each ESA. Mention that the ESA is an opportunity to confirm quality via the assurance roles.

- You get more than half the marks for relating your answer to the scenario and less than half for copying the generic point straight from the manual, i.e. can you show how the point would be applied to this situation?

- Don't repeat yourself. Each point only carries a certain number of marks. Repeating something three or four times throughout the answer does not increase the number of marks. If you have a point to make, say everything about it once, then leave it alone.

- Diagrams are perfectly acceptable. Remember that a title in a diagram may not say everything about it that is needed (When, why etc.). A diagram copied from the manual may earn some marks, but it is likely that the question is asking you to tune it to the scenario.

The Problems

Since the introduction of the PRINCE 2 Professional Examinations in January 1997, most of the failures have stemmed from the Practitioner Exam. The reasons are varied. Some candidates simply run out of time and fail to score sufficient marks for the final question. But most fail because they are unable to make the all-important connections between the Scenario, the Question, their Experience and the PRINCE 2 Method. There is usually little doubt that the candidates understand the Method, proven by the relatively low failure rate in the Foundation Exam (less than 5%) which tests knowledge of PRINCE 2, and the majority are sensible middle-managers with at least some practical experience of project management. So the conclusion is that the problems lie with:

- time management

- information retrieval

- examination technique.

Time Management

The requirement for passing the Practitioner Examination is that you must score at least 50% of the marks available. With 50 marks available for each of the three questions, a total of 75 marks must be achieved to pass the exam. The marks are averaged over all the questions so it is possible (but difficult) to compensate for a poorly answered question elsewhere in the paper.

Marks Scored

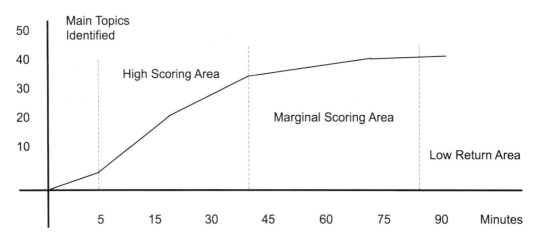

The main problem is that an early answer scoring low marks cannot possibly be compensated for in the final question if you run out of time and are unable to complete the final question. This seems an obvious statement but is a common occurrence!

The remedy is to ensure that the best use is made of the time available; a reasonable approach is that 50 - 55 minutes should be allocated to each question. This should enable you sufficient time to score around 40 marks per question which is about as many as you can reasonably expect under examination conditions.

Most marks will be scored during the first part of the answer - typically the content written after the first 5 minutes and before the end of 45 minutes. On this basis you should start a new question after writing for no longer than 50 minutes.

Always begin a new question on a separate sheet and number each answer sheet individually - *Question 1 - Sheet 1* etc. This will enable you to return to your answer and add additional content during the final 15 minutes or so of the exam. Although it might seem to be potentially confusing and time-wasting having to pick up momentum again on each question, the PRINCE 2 Method is so inherently integrated that you are almost bound to recall additional key points as you tackle the other questions. Don't expect to pick up too many additional marks but even one or two extra marks might help and you might just identify something significant that you failed to cover during the first pass.

Always leave time to read through your work. This will disclose missing references and possibly missing key points. Allow about 15 minutes for this - if you find any major omissions and don't have time to write up the full text just bullet-point the key features and you will be given marks for including them.

Information Retrieval

A problem often encountered when preparing for the exam is the identification of the key points that form the structure of the answer. The options open are:

1. To simply "Brain-Dump" all the related topics onto a sheet;

2. To go through the Contents Sheet of the PRINCE 2 Manual and identify all relevant topics;

3. To select the appropriate Components, Processes or Techniques referred to in the question and extract the information directly from the appropriate Chapters in the PRINCE 2 Manual;

4. To do something more speedy and productive than any of the above!

The Brain-Dump Approach

This technique assumes that you have sufficient knowledge of the subject matter and the ability to retrieve the most important parts. Some people have this ability and find the technique fast and accurate enough to pass the exam - unfortunately most don't!

Brain-dumping is by its nature unstructured and "hit and miss" for most of us; lots of fairly irrelevant points, reflecting our own feelings and experiences always surface and they invariably take a lot of time to write down and sort into some sort of logical order and priority. Unless you are well practised, avoid this approach.

The Contents Sheet Approach

The PRINCE 2 Manual Contents Sheet addresses the whole of the Method and is an excellent full reference. Unfortunately its very comprehensiveness works against it as a technique for preparing for the examination as the time taken to work through the 14 A4 sides of Contents Sheet is time consuming and unexciting.

To use this technique, ensure that you have a clear view of what you are seeking - essentially a "scope" - otherwise you might just end up re-writing the whole contents each time you address a question! Write the main topic being interrogated at the top of your answer paper and list the bullet-points (and possibly page references) underneath. You will need to be very focused to ensure that only relevant key points are identified; aim for 12- 20 key topic points.

Referring to the Contents Sheet is a useful way to check your list of topics produced by other methods. A quick scan can deliver additional relevant points and help your confidence levels.

Using the PRINCE 2 Manual to Identify the Key Topics

This is the most time-consuming approach and has inherent dangers, the chief being that it is all too easy to become focused on just one topic area and ignore the all-important scenario spin-offs that will earn the marks you need to pass the exam.

The examiner is looking for a demonstration that you understand the elements of the PRINCE 2 Method and are able to apply it to the given scenario, at the same time addressing the question. It is all too easy to become bogged down in the detail of a particular topic and omit references to other associated elements.

For example, if the question asks how PRINCE 2 Quality aspects can contribute to a scenario where the Customer has concerns about Quality, the answer must address not only the rather obvious "Quality In A Project Environment" Component but who has responsibility - the "Organisation" Component and the Role Descriptions in Appendix C of the PRINCE 2 Manual. Also the means of achieving quality ("Work Packages" in the "Controlling A Stage" and "Managing Product Delivery" Processes). Obviously the "Quality Review" Technique and the connections with "Product Descriptions" and their "Quality Criteria" must also be established, described and discussed in the context of the set scenario. To identify all these major topic areas (and a number of others not mentioned) would take a considerable time going through the PRINCE 2 Manual; certainly more time than is available in the three hour exam!

But the key topics must be identified, and pre-exam preparation to pull out the relevant key topic areas will help on the day. Remember you are allowed to take any notes you make during your preparation and any training event notes and documentation you possess into the exam - so time taken in advance will be well spent.

An Alternative Approach

If you have followed the guidance in this booklet, during your preparation for the Foundation Exam, you will have prepared both high-level and in-depth "Process Maps" showing all the major Processes and Processes, and the related flows of Management and Quality Products.

You can use your high-level Process Map to follow the normal route of a project picking up the PRINCE 2 topic headings you are searching for. Each time you identify a relationship between a PRINCE 2 Process Flow and a topic heading you should note down the topic heading which will be used as the basis for writing your answer. You should aim for about 12-20 topic areas, which when integrated and combined will give you 6-8 key paragraph headings. Spend no more than 5 minutes on this exercise, especially if using it during the PRINCE 2 exam. Using the example Question Paper, the following Topics might well be identified using this approach:

Customer Quality Concerns - Key Points:

1. Customer Quality Expectations
2. Organisation - Project Board; Senior User
3. User/Customer Involvement
4. Project Assurance
5. Planning for Quality
6. Configuration Management
7. Quality Log
8. Work Packages; Project Manager & Team Manager Agreement
9. Quality Reviews & QR Technique
10. Product Descriptions
11. Quality Criteria
12. Feedback
    - Highlight Reports
    - Checkpoint Reports
    - ESAs

Once the main topic areas have been identified, the answer can be written up by reference to "Bullet Points" supported by short explanations; remember the Examiner will be trying to spot the main answer scheme topics and then judge the extent to which you have provided a full answer with reference to the question and scenario.

All questions stand alone. If a point comes up in a question which you have already made in answer to an earlier question make it again - do not refer back to a previous answer.

Structuring Your Answer

The marking scheme used by the examiner has already been described. Being able to retrieve all the relevant information will not necessarily result in a pass paper. This is because about two thirds of the marks awarded relate to the Candidate's ability to apply the PRINCE 2 elements identified to the particular scenario. To maximise your mark collecting, your answer to each of the three questions should aim to reflect this marking approach.

You have two basic options when actually writing your answer - the following diagrams and text illustrate this:

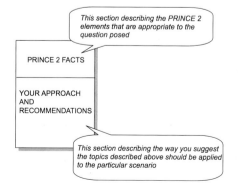

- Using the Checklist suggested for the example question on Quality, group together related topics to produce 6-8 main paragraph headings.

- Plan to roughly split each answer into two - one third explaining the PRINCE 2 elements that apply and two thirds relating those elements to the scenario.

This is the simplest way to produce your answer - it enables a clear separation between factual information available from the PRINCE 2 Manual and your thoughts about applying those elements to the question and the scenario.

Its main disadvantage is that each identified element has to be visited twice - once to explain the PRINCE 2 point and again to show how you would apply that point to the particular scenario. The benefit of this approach lies mainly in its lack of structural complexity which may well prove a boon under anxious examination conditions!

An example of this approach is shown below - the answer is not a complete answer to a full question but an extract taken to illustrate the planning, writing approach and style.

> *Example Scenario: A database migration project with a very tight timescale and management concerns that delays will lead to significant loss of business.*
>
> *Question: Explain how PRINCE 2 may be used to identify and manage the risk.*
>
> ## *Topics Identified:*
>
> *1. Risk Log - creation, use, up-date*
>
> *2. Risk Analysis - Identification, Estimation, Evaluation*
>
> *3. Risk Actions - Prevention, Transfer, Accept etc*
>
> *4. Risk Management - Planning, Resourcing, Monitor, Control*
>
> *5. Business Risk:Project Risk*
>
> *6. Stage Boundaries - minimum up-date - ESA*
>
> *7. Communication - Checkpoint, Highlight Reports*
>
> *Risk is defined as ... "the chance of exposure to the adverse consequences of future events" (PRINCE 2 Manual 8.2). The PRINCE 2 elements that apply to this question are:*
>
> ### *Risk Log*
> *PRINCE 2 requires that the Component "Management of Risk" be applied to every project. Risks are first identified in the "Starting Up A Project" Process (SU4) where the Project Brief is created and the Risk Log is created to capture these initial risks. The Risk Log is used to capture and track the progress of risks as the project proceeds. The initial Risk Log is refined in "Initiating A Project" Process (IP3 - Refining The Business Case & Risks) where a full Risk Analysis will be carried out, and up-dated, minimally, when the Risk Analysis is re-visited in the "Managing Stage Boundaries" Process where the preparatory work for the End Stage Assessment (ESA) is carried out.*
>
> ### *Risk Analysis:*
> *There are three steps recommended by PRINCE 2 for Risk Analysis (PRINCE Manual 8.4.1):*
>
> *Risk Identification - capturing the potential risks;*
>
> *Risk Estimation - measuring the likelihood and impact of each identified risk;*
>
> *Risk Evaluation - assessing whether any of the risks are acceptable or what action is necessary for management of the risk.*
>
> ### *Risk Actions (PRINCE Manual 8.4.1):*
> *Where Risk Evaluation shows up a significant risk one or more of the following actions might be appropriate:*

Prevention - *to attempt to stop the risk happening;*

Reduction - *reducing the likelihood and/or impact;*

Transfer - *passing on the risk to a third party - often at a financial cost;*

Contingency - *putting into place a series of actions should the risk materialise;*

Acceptance - *cautious commitment, hoping that the risk may not materialise.*

Risk Management:

Once actions to counter the identified risks have been decided the risks must be managed. This is achieved by **Planning** *and* **Resourcing** *the risk countermeasures. The plan must then be* **Monitored** *and* **Controlled** *to ensure that early warning is assured and that action is taken to put the countermeasures into effect (PRINCE Manual 8.4.2).*

... end of the "PRINCE 2 Topics" section of the answer ...

———————————————————————————————

... start of the "Application to the Scenario" section of the answer ...

Risk Log

I recommend that a Project Brief be produced and a Risk Log be established. To achieve this I recommend a short meeting between the Project Manager, the Senior User (or User Assurance nominee) the Supplier representative and the Executive (or Business Assurance nominee) where an Initial Risk Analysis will point out the immediate and obvious risks facing the project. To record this I recommend that a Risk Log be created and that it be up-dated when the Risk Analysis is refined during the creation of the Draft Project Initiation Document. Subsequently I recommend that the Risk Analysis and the Risk Log be updated, minimally, at the end of each Management Stage in preparation for the Project Board's End Stage Assessment. In addition to this I recommend that the Risk Analysis be reviewed on a weekly basis for the first month, and the Risk Log up-dated, because of the Management concerns about schedule delay coupled with the substantial negative impact a schedule delay would cause.

Risk Analysis:

All three suggested steps of Risk Analysis must be carried out. Under **Risk Identification** *it is likely that schedule delay and loss of existing and new business will be major risks identified.* **Risk Estimation** *must be carefully measured in this case as the impact on the Company is likely to be substantial; I recommend that specialist Supplier and Business resources be involved at a formal Risk Analysis Workshop to ensure all the relevant information is available. I recommend that the acceptability of each identified risk be formally considered by the Project Board prior to any commercial decision being taken. Each Project Board member must have the opportunity to input to* **Risk Evaluation** *and a formal meeting, towards the end of the Risk Workshop, is recommended. To help their deliberations I recommend that proper metrics be used for Risk Analysis and a "threshold" figure for an "unacceptable level of risk" be established and agreed.*

Risk Actions:

Clear decisions about what is and is not an acceptable risk must be followed up by a statement of what the Project Manager's recommendations are and confirmation of Project Board support. I recommend that the Project Board's decisions be recorded and that a physical sign-off is obtained. In this scenario, the high Business Risks make it unlikely that any major risks would be "accepted" without some action being proposed. A more pro-active approach is necessary with transference and/or sharing of risks with the new supplier being attractive; in any event contingency planning must be put into place.

Risk Management:

A properly resourced plan, signed up to by the Project Board (and published to all the Project Management team) must be prepared as soon as possible after Risk Actions have been agreed. The risks must be monitored at least every week and the risk plan up-dated. Any change in circumstance (schedule or resource) must be picked up and reported to the Project Board. A Tolerance on risk should be introduced to provide a "trigger" for when such reference should occur.

Notice how the answer focuses specifically on PRINCE 2 for the first part and that, having covered all the major topics, then expands on the answer by applying the identified PRINCE 2 elements to the scenario and question. Note also that the answer, as far as it goes, reflects the suggested one third/two thirds rule.

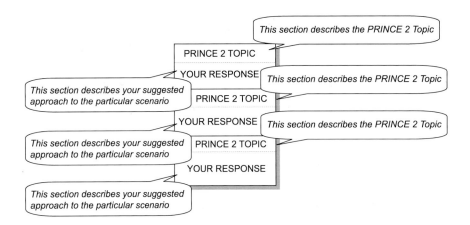

A more refined answer, requiring only one visit to each of the topics is summarised by this diagram. Each identified topic is described in respect of its PRINCE 2 aspect, followed by recommendations on usage within the specific scenario. An example portion of answer for the same scenario and question, using the same text is illustrated as follows:

Risk is defined as ... "the chance of exposure to the adverse consequences of future events". The PRINCE 2 Elements that apply to this question are:

Risk Log

PRINCE 2 requires that the Component "Management of Risk" be applied to every project. Risks are first identified in the "Starting Up A Project" Process (SU4) where the Project Brief is created and the Risk Log is created to capture these initial risks.

I recommend that a Project Brief be produced and a Risk Log be established. To achieve this I recommend a short meeting between the Project Manager, the Senior User (or User Assurance nominee) the Supplier representative and the Executive (or Business Assurance nominee) where an Initial Risk Analysis will point out the immediate and obvious risks facing the project. To record this I recommend that a Risk Log be created and that it be up-dated when the Risk Analysis is refined during the creation of the Draft Project Initiation Document.

The Risk Log is used to capture and track the progress of risks as the project proceeds. The initial Risk Log is refined in "Initiating A Project" Process (IP3 - Refining The Business Case & Risks) where a full Risk Analysis will be carried out, and up-dated, minimally, when the Risk Analysis is re-visited in the "Managing Stage Boundaries" Process where the preparatory work for the End Stage Assessment (ESA) is carried out.

I recommend that the Risk Analysis and the Risk Log be updated, minimally, at the end of each Management Stage in preparation for the Project Board's End

Stage Assessment. In addition to this I recommend that the Risk Analysis be reviewed on a weekly basis for the first month, and the Risk Log up-dated, because of the Management concerns about schedule delay coupled with the substantial negative impact a schedule delay would cause.

How Not To Answer A Question!

So far this book has discussed the positive aspects of preparing for the exam and has given advice on identifying the main topics to be addressed.

Later on there are specimen answers to the question set at the beginning of this Section showing an appropriate style and approach which should prove to be very useful.

There is, however, some mileage in providing an example of how **not** to write an answer! The following example is taken from a Candidate's paper and illustrates an answer that scored very few marks - you are advised to read it and then completely erase it from your memory!

Question - "How would you use (if at all) the "Controlling A Stage (CS)" and "Managing Product Delivery (MP)" Processes in a small project?

The Controlled Stage approach which PRINCE 2 adopts would be relevant for a small project - ie Controlled Start, Controlled Progress and Controlled Close as this would:

- *Ensure that the viability of the project was continually being assessed;*

- *That the End Stage Assessments were carried out to enable important decisions to be made before more detailed work was carried out;*

- *Clarify impact of external events.*

In a small project the Initiation Stage and Start Up could be combined as a Controlled Start. The Project Initiation Stage is comparatively short and inexpensive but is essential in order to:

- *Define the Project Objectives and how they will be met;*

- *Clearly understand and state the Business Case;*

- *Identify who the Customer is;*

- *Outline Responsibilities and Authority;*

- *Determine Project Boundaries;*

- *Document any Assumptions that have been made;*

- *Identify any Risks which may prevent the Project from achieving a successful outcome;*

- *Determine when the Major Products will be delivered;*

- *Determine Costs;*

- *Determine Controls;*

- *Determine the Stages of the Project;*

- *Determine Quality Assurance.*

At the end of the Project Initiation Stage, the Project Initiation Document would be produced, covering all these questions and this would then become the reference document to show the original basis for the project.

As the end of a Stage is a major control point for the Project Board, having gone through the Initiation Stage they would have been in a position to decide whether to continue with the project before incurring any more costs.

The answer to the question is reproduced exactly as presented to the examiner. A simple analysis of content reveals lack of reference to PRINCE 2, incorrect terminology and no explanation for each element of *what it is, when it is introduced into the project lifecycle, the purpose it serves* and *how it works*. The original question was set within a scenario; the answer provides no linkage or cross-reference to the scenario; taken in isolation, there is no way of assessing what the original scenario might have been.

ANSWER Q's

EACH PRINCE ELEMENT

1 WHAT IT IS
2 WHEN IS IT INTRODUCED TO PROJECT
3 ITS PURPOSE
4 HOW IT WORKS
5 DERIVATION

Specimen Answers

Specimen answers have been prepared for the three questions posed in the example paper at the beginning of this Section and they are reproduced on the following pages. The original answers were all produced under examination conditions and some timings have been shown; the key topics that would score marks are shown in italics - generally 1 mark would be earned for each topic although some are repeated and would not score twice! The examiners have discretion to award bonus marks.

PRINCE 2 Practitioner Examination

Question 1: Customer concerns about Quality

Key Points:

1. Customer Quality Expectations
2. Organisation - Project Board; Senior User
3. User/Customer Involvement
4. Project Assurance
5. Planning for Quality
6. Configuration Management
7. Quality Log
8. Work Packages; Project Manager & Team Manager Agreement
9. Quality Reviews & QR Technique
10. Product Descriptions
11. Quality Criteria
12. Feedback
    – Highlight Reports
    – Checkpoint Reports
    – ESAs

ITALICS = MARKS

Customer Quality Expectations

Within a PRINCE 2 project, quality must be *planned from the start*. The quality of the End Product and the individual Products that make up the finally delivered outcome will be based on the stated *"Customer's Quality Expectations"*. These might be identified in the trigger for the project - the *Project Mandate* (see Appendix A.19) but, as the Project Mandate might take almost any form, this cannot be counted upon. In any event the Customer's Quality Expectations will be included in the *Project Brief* (Appendix A.16).

In this particular project, a *clear statement* of the Customer's Quality Expectations must be established so that all concerned can *clearly understand exactly what quality issues need to be addressed when planning the project and evaluating the delivered Products.*

Planning for Quality

The Customer's Quality Expectations will be used, together with information about the Organisation's (and possibly the Suppliers') *Quality Management System*, the Project Brief, and the Project Approach, to *plan for quality during the "Initiating A Project Process" (IP1)* and to produce the project's *Quality Plan.*

This is essential in this scenario where there is obviously real anxiety within the Customer organisation about quality aspects; Quality Planning must be seen to be done and carried out. It is recommended that *full Customer involvement in creating the Quality Plan is implemented* and that *the Senior User (representing the customers at Project Board level) be asked to nominate a suitable representative* to contribute to, and give commitment to, planning for quality.

Quality Reviews & QR Technique

In PRINCE 2, and appropriate to the project in the scenario, the *main means of achieving* and confirming the required and *expected level of quality* is the *Quality Review* (one of the PRINCE 2 *Techniques*). This enables each Product (or Deliverable) to be *measured against its Product Description* especially the stated, agreed and published *Quality Criteria. All Products must be measured against their Quality Criteria, using whatever method is judged to be the most sensible* in the circumstances (this will be recorded in the Product Description). The QR Technique may be used *informally* (for example, a desk check or inspection or test) or *formally* via a meeting where selected Reviewers (people who can make a contribution to assessing the Product) meet to identify *potential errors, inconsistencies and omissions for follow-up action*

For this project, I would recommend that the *Formal Quality Review Technique be used for all Products*, especially those where there has been a poor quality track record or where the User is particularly sensitive. This would *provide confidence* that all Products meet their stated Quality Criteria. *The Senior User should be asked to nominate suitably experienced staff to represent the customer's interests as Reviewers for Quality Reviews.*

The following *diagram summarises the QR Technique within PRINCE 2 and illustrates how I recommend the scenario project's Products should be measured against their Quality Criteria*:

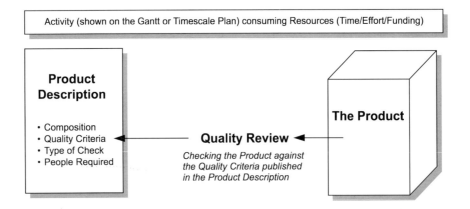

Product Descriptions

A *Product Description is created for each Project-level and Stage-level Product* to specify and define its Content and Quality Criteria. The Product Description is *baselined when the plan it relates to is baselined by agreement from the Project Board (or Project Manager/Team Manager in the case of Team Plans)* and must not be omitted from a PRINCE 2 project for any reason. *It will form an essential part of the Work Package Authorisation.*

The full content for a Product Description is included in the PRINCE 2 manual in the "Product Based Planning" Technique and is *summarised as follows: Product Title, Purpose, Composition, Derivation, Format and Presentation, Allocated To, Quality Criteria, Type of Check Required, People & skills required for reviewing/testing the Product.*

Work Packages; Project Manager & Team Manager Agreement

A *Product Description is always included in the Work Package* (See Appendix A.26) produced by the Project Manager (in CS1) and *agreed with the Team Manager* (or individual responsible for creating the Product) in MP1. *A Work Package is effectively the "contract"* between the Project Manager and Team Manager (or individual) for creation of the Product - it *will provide agreement* on (Checkpoint) reporting, timescale, delivery of the completed Work Package etc. providing for a *clear and unambiguous understanding of the quality requirements for the Product.*

In the scenario, the use of Product Descriptions, in conjunction with the Work Package, will be *essential to control the work of the sub-contractors and will provide the means to secure the required level of quality* (ie the Quality Criteria) without excessive "hands-on" work by the Project Manager. *Involvement of the Senior User's nominee(s) and/or User Project Assurance representative(s) will help create more effective Product Descriptions and Work Packages and help manage the User Management concerns about quality.*

Quality Criteria

These are included in the Product Description for each product and are the *means against which the Product will be measured as a "quality Product".* Quality Criteria should be *measurable* where possible and *agreed with the people responsible* for creating the Product before work commences.

For the project in the scenario I recommend that the setting of Quality Criteria for all major Products (especially those that are "Customer-Facing" and/or on the Critical Path) be *a joint activity between the Project Manager, the Team Manager and the Customer.* For the Customer input, the *Senior User should be asked to nominate suitable staff with the appropriate knowledge of the Customer's Quality Expectations to make a full contribution.*

Organisation - Project Board; Senior User; User/Customer Involvement

The *quality concerns of the customer can be managed by planning for full involvement of customer staff in the Quality Review process* described above. A PRINCE 2 project would always have a Project Board which will include *Senior User representation* (see the Organisation Component). The Senior User will be in a position to *commit and deliver user/customer resources for ensuring quality* by *nominating suitable Quality Reviewers* and by *being involved in Planning Quality (IP1), creation of the Quality Plan (IP1) and being party to the agreement of Work Packages (MP1) (via the nominated User Assurance resource).*

For the project in the scenario *I would ensure that the User Management who have the concerns about quality and timely delivery, take on the role of Senior User(s) or, if they are not able to provide sufficient time, that a suitably authorised and senior representative is appointed on their behalf. Very busy Senior Users will be reassured that "all is well" with the project (especially the quality and schedule aspects which they are worried about) by appointing a User Assurance representative to look after these matters on a day-to-day basis.*

Feedback - Checkpoint Reports

The Quality Reviews will be carried out in MP2; they will not always be performed at the conclusion of a Work Package or Product but may, where appropriate, be carried out part way through. *Reports on how the plan (and the quality aspects) is proceeding* can and should be reported to the Project Manager via *Checkpoint Reports* (generated in MP2). Checkpoint Reports will be raised by the Team Manager in the *format and at the frequency agreed in the Work Package* (see MP1 17.4.3 and the Controls Component 6.4.8).

In this particular project, I recommend that *Checkpoint Reports be produced following an informal meeting with the Team Manager, the Team resources and the User Assurance nominee; frequency of Checkpoints and the associated reports should be weekly.*

Feedback - Quality Log

A Quality Log will also be established to keep track of the quality checks planned and achieved for each Product (see Appendix A.22). In this project, the Quality Log should *be included with the Senior User's copy of the Highlight Report* as further evidence of the control of quality.

Feedback - Highlight Reports

The Project Manager uses the *information from the Checkpoint Reports to reflect progress made against the Stage Plan* (CS2 - Assessing Progress) and to use the resultant information to Review Stage Status (CS5) *prior to reporting progress to Project Board members via a Highlight Report* (CS6).

In the scenario situation, focus within the Highlight Reports on the Quality aspects will help *manage the concerns of the Senior User representing the User/Customer interests.*

Feedback - End Stage Assessments (ESAs)

At the end of each *Management Stage, when a decision has to be taken on whether to approve the project's progress into the next Stage. Reports on Product Quality* from the current Stage can easily be derived from the Highlight Reports (A.9), Checkpoint Reports (A.3), Quality Log (A.22), *Issue Log (A.10) (Project Issues will be raised to record any errors or quality discrepancies with the Products),* and Quality Review Sign-offs (see the Quality Review Technique) to present a complete *"quality picture"* to the Senior User and help in the decision making process.

For the project, the ESA is an essential control and *the End Stage Report generated in the "Managing Stage Boundaries (SB)" Process* should be drawn to reflect the Customer's quality concerns from the reports described above. *The ESA Agenda will include presentation and discussion of Quality Management and the User Assurance nominee asked to produce a separate, quality focused, report to the whole Project Board.*

Project Assurance

The Senior User will be able to be assured of the reality and truthfulness of the information presented by *appointing a (user) Project Assurance representative* to ensure/assure that everything on the project was as presented. However, *User Assurance is, and remains, the ultimate responsibility of the Senior User* (see Appendix C.3.1) and *cannot be delegated to the Project Manager.*

As described above, a User Assurance nominee should be appointed for this project to reassure the Senior User (and the rest of the Project Board) that the correct procedures are being observed and that "all is well".

Configuration Management (CM)

The overall situation on completed (ie Quality Reviewed and signed-off) Products will be tracked by *Configuration Management* (possibly run by a Configuration Librarian or Project Support if appointed). This allows any *quality problems arising from MP2 to be tracked back to source* and remedial action taken. Project Assurance would keep an eye on this. For this project (and any PRINCE 2 project), *Configuration Management is not optional* - I recommend that the *User Assurance nominee be tasked to monitor the proper use of CM especially where there are Products where problems were being encountered.*

In summary, the user can be confident that the correct and sensible application of PRINCE 2 to a project where quality is of concern, will help manage anxieties and provide a suitable end result of the required quality.

PRINCE 2 Practitioner Examination

Question 2 - Product Breakdown Structure, Product Flow Diagram, Product Description

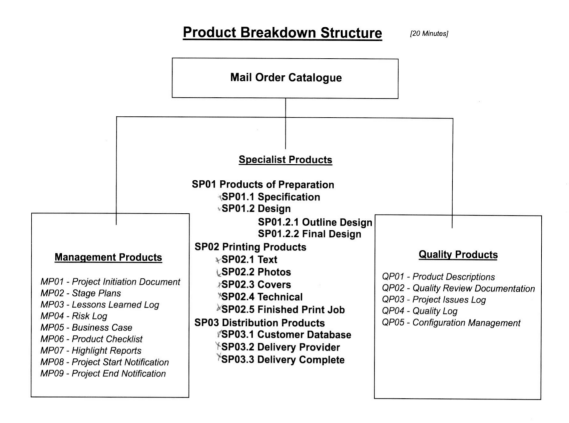

Product Breakdown Structure   [20 Minutes]

Mail Order Catalogue

Specialist Products

SP01 Products of Preparation
 SP01.1 Specification
 SP01.2 Design
  SP01.2.1 Outline Design
  SP01.2.2 Final Design
SP02 Printing Products
 SP02.1 Text
 SP02.2 Photos
 SP02.3 Covers
 SP02.4 Technical
 SP02.5 Finished Print Job
SP03 Distribution Products
 SP03.1 Customer Database
 SP03.2 Delivery Provider
 SP03.3 Delivery Complete

Management Products

MP01 - Project Initiation Document
MP02 - Stage Plans
MP03 - Lessons Learned Log
MP04 - Risk Log
MP05 - Business Case
MP06 - Product Checklist
MP07 - Highlight Reports
MP08 - Project Start Notification
MP09 - Project End Notification

Quality Products

QP01 - Product Descriptions
QP02 - Quality Review Documentation
QP03 - Project Issues Log
QP04 - Quality Log
QP05 - Configuration Management

Note: Not all the Management and Quality Products that would be applicable to a "full" PRINCE 2 project are shown in the above PBS - I have selected those I believe to be essential for proper project management and control and would agree this selection with the Project Board.

Product Flow Diagram Mail Order Catalogue

[15 Minutes]

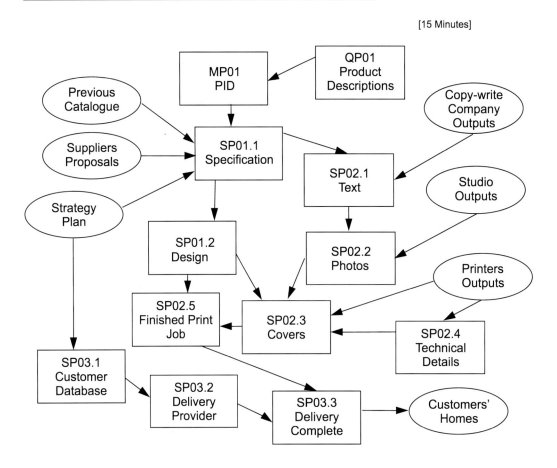

Please note that it is neither appropriate nor helpful to include all the Management and Quality Products onto the Product Flow Diagram. The above diagram includes the PID (a Management Product) and Product Descriptions (Quality Products) as these would be appropriate and helpful to include for planning purposes. Other Management Products (eg Checkpoint Reports, Highlight reports), and Quality Products (eg Project issues, Quality Reviews) do not fit easily into the structure and would risk causing some confusion; they have, therefore, been deliberately omitted from the diagram.

Product Description [20 Minutes]

Product Title: Covers - Ref S.2.3

Purpose: To provide an attractive, protective cover for the Mail Order Catalogue.

Composition:
Front Cover:
– Company Name
– Company Logo
– Catalogue Name
– Photo(s)
– Date/Period Covered

Back Cover:
– Company Information
– Telephone
– Address
– Hotline No For Assistance
– Photo(s)

Derivation: Photo Studio; Product S.1.2 Design

Format & Presentation: Glossy, 200 gsm. Company Standard 123

Allocated To: D. Smith - Sales

Quality Criteria:
1: At least 2mm overlap of Catalogue Contents
2: Reflects Company style and image
3: At least one photo on front cover

Type of Quality Check: Formal Quality Review by Project Manager, Head of Marketing, and External Design Company representative

People or Skills Required: Bob Jones - Design Consultant
Andy Smith - Head of Marketing
Roger Black - Marketing Manager

The PRINCE 2 Manual (Product-Based Planning Technique 21.3.1) contains an explanation of the Headings in the Product Description

PRINCE 2 Practitioner Examination

Question 3 - Stages

Key Topics:

1. What Control is about

2. What Stages Are

3. Management/Technical Stages

4. How Stages are used

5. Who is the Main user of Stages

6. How to define the stages for the project

7. Suggested Stages for the project   [5 mins]

What Control Is About

All projects need to be properly controlled to ensure that the Business Benefits will be delivered through the completion of the project's outcome on time, within budget and meeting the agreed requirements. The PRINCE 2 concept of defining Stages and the associated reviews at their beginning and at their conclusion *(End Stage Assessments - ESAs) are key controls in achieving effective control.*

What Stages Are

A major feature of the control of any project is *to break down the overall project into a number of manageable Stages*; these Stages *are partitions of the project with decision points.* This enables managers with decision making responsibilities (in PRINCE 2 called the *"Project Board") to release the resources* (effort, time and money) on a *"limited commitment" basis rather than agree to and commit to everything up front.* This approach also enables two further features:

- Overall *approval in principle to the total project* (with the overall project being planned largely in outline);

- *Firm commitment of the next Stage of the work* (with the next Stage being planned in detail in terms of Products (Deliverables), Effort required, Timescale, and Cost).

How Stages Are Used

End Stage Assessments (ESAs) enable the Project Board to consider, formally, how well the project is performing against its agreed baseline plan and to *ensure that the Products are as required and to their stated Quality Criteria.*

ESAs provide *decision points at either end of each Stage* giving a "commitment and review" concept for the project. (PRINCE 2 Manual 7.2.2). Each Stage comprises the Products (or Deliverables) and the resources (time, cost and effort) needed to achieve them. Senior management in the form of the "Project Board" is then able to control the release of these resources at the key, *event related decision points* usually in the form of an ESA meeting (see the PRINCE 2 Manual Controls Component 6.4.13).

The Main User Of Stages

PRINCE 2 is driven by 8 Processes (see Chapter 12) and commitment of resources to each Management Stage is carried out in the *"Directing A Project (DP)"* Process (see Chapter 15 (especially DP1 and DP3). The DP Process is owned by the Project Board and is the main authorisation and approval Process. The Project Board comprises three functional roles - The Senior User, the Senior Supplier and the Executive - this ensures that the right people are being involved in the key decision making elements of the project right from the start and throughout the project.

Management/Technical Stages

Management Stages are used to commit resources and give authority to spend as described above (see 7.3). There will also, typically, be *Technical Stages* nesting within each Management Stage. Technical Stages are *typified by the use of particular sets of Specialist (or technical) skills. Management Stages will always run in series - never in parallel.* Technical Stages, however will usually run in parallel and usually be planned that way. They may also run over the boundaries of Management Stages.

The following diagram illustrates this concept:

	Management Stage 1		Management Stage 2			Management Stage 3				Management Stage 4		
Specification												
Design	Technical Stage											
Contract												
Build					Technical Stage							
Test							Technical Stage					
Install										Technical Stage		

Responsibility for each Management Stage will fall to the Project Manager, but *management of Technical Stages will normally be the responsibility of a "Team Manager"* (see 4.2.6 and Appendix C). Team Managers will sometimes be the contractors receiving formal orders - it is up to them to plan and control the Technical Stage work and the work carried out by their own resources. They will *agree the resultant, detailed, plan with the Project Manager* allowing the Project Manager to keep focused on each Management Stage *rather than doing all the work!*

Defining The Stages For The Project

End Stage Assessments will be held to consider what has been achieved, its impact on the project and Business Case and the next Stage; this is all prepared for in "Managing Stage Boundaries" (SB). *A Stage boundary should always be placed at a major "milestone"* where one or more significant Products have been produced and a sensible and informed decision on continuing with the project can be made.

Suggested Stages For The Project in the Scenario

Suggested Stages for the project are shown on the following page. Note that the stage reviews (ESAs) are planned at *key decision points,* when major deliverables are scheduled for completion. The Activities/Technical Stages in each Management Stage would be derived from *the Product Flow Diagram* (see the PRINCE 2 Manual - Product Based Planning "Identifying Activities & Dependencies" (PL3)) and agreed with the Project Board for them to commit the necessary resources for the project. *Consideration should be given to appointing a Team Manager for each major area of specialist activity* (Technical Stages) to plan the work to a more detailed level.

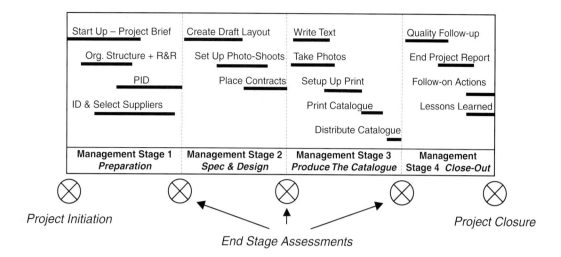

Author's/Examiner's Note: some key topics are omitted from this answer - the main marks-scoring topics missing are:

- Cautious commitment in high-risk situations (up to 3 marks)

- Management by exception - Exception Reports (up to 3 marks)

- Exception Plans + Mid Stage Assessments (up to 3 marks)

- Tolerance - Standard Time & Cost (up to 4 marks)

- Minimum of 2 Management Stages - Initiation being the first (up to 2 marks)

- Review of "actuals" against the agreed plan (up to 2 marks)

About the Answer Script Generally: This is a generally good script which would certainly pass the PRINCE 2 Practitioner Examination. Question 1 has been answered very thoroughly and would attract very good marks (40+). The Question 2 response is an excellent example of how to answer this type of question with diagrams (the main requirement) and some explanatory text to explain the approach (and deliberate omissions); answer 2 would score near maximum marks - at least 45. Question 3 has seemingly suffered from the time spent answering the first two questions - this is not uncommon! About one third of the available marks have not been addressed and the answer is effectively being marked out of a possible 33 marks. Remember, however, that the Examiner has discretion to award bonus marks and the answer, as far as it goes, is good and can be expected to attract at least the 25 marks required for a pass (remember that the marks for all three answers are aggregated and you must achieve 50% overall - 75 marks out of a possible 150). The example answer script ends up as a respectable pass paper, scoring around 110 marks.

Note that the style of answer for Questions 1 and 3 are different, reflecting the styles discussed earlier in this book. The Question 1 response handles the Candidates views and recommendations for the project in the scenario as the answer progresses - a helpful style for the Examiner who can see clearly that the Candidate understands the PRINCE 2 element and is then able to relate it to the given scenario. This approach is straightforward and successful; if you adopt it try dividing each bullet point into thirds - one third to describe the PRINCE 2 element and the remaining two thirds relating the point to the scenario project.

The response to question 3 takes a different tack, dividing the answer into two parts; the Candidate has described the PRINCE concept of Stages (as the question asked) and then moved onto the second part describing how Stages would be used in the scenario project. This is an acceptable approach but is dangerous for the third answer where time might well be running out. The highest mark-scoring zone in the examination is where the Candidate relates the topic to the scenario - in the specimen answer there is relatively little written on this! The approach might also be a little more difficult for the Examiner as the marking scheme will have to be visited twice, at different times; this might (or might not) work in the Candidate's favour.

Close Out

If you've managed to get this far you are as ready for the PRINCE 2 Examinations as you are ever likely to be. It remains only to wish you the little bit of luck that we all need to make a success of any venture in life. If you are still not confident of your knowledge of PRINCE 2 or your ability to convince an examiner that you are able to apply it to a given situation, you should consider attending an APM Group accredited training event and, perhaps, try to gain a little more experience in using the Method.

Practising writing answers to typical project management situations, using the approaches suggested in this book will certainly help to prepare you for the exam and help develop your ability to respond to a problem using a structured method.

The scenario for which the specimen answers have been prepared can also be used to practise writing further answers - for example *"Design a suitable Project Management Team for the project"* and *"Identify five risks and say what steps you would take to handle them"*.

The examination scenario and questions on the next page can also be used; try to identify the key topics for each question first; then answer the questions (or at least some parts of them). Remembering that you will not score all the marks for just identifying and explaining the PRINCE topic, but that you must relate the topic to the scenario, measure your answer against the marking scheme - this, after all, is exactly what the examiner will be doing!

Good luck

Appendix 1

Example Examination Question & Marking Scheme

The APM Group have provided the Accredited Training Organisations with an example Question Paper and Marking Scheme; these are included on the following pages and are well worth studying as they provide a useful insight into the Examiner's approach to marking your paper.

A colleague who works for a large leisure group has been given the job of Project Manager for a major refurbishment of a large hotel. He has no project management training and the company does not have project management standards. He wants your advice on a number of topics.

One point which worries him is that there will be several contractors to handle the different specialities, such as plumbing, building, decoration, pool refurbishment and others. He has no idea how to plan or control such an undertaking. Remember in all your answers that he has no knowledge of PRINCE 2.

Keep your answers brief. Flowing text is not required. Write just enough to show that you understand what should be used, its purpose, who would use it and when.

1. *How would you suggest that he approach the planning of the project? Make brief notes explaining how PRINCE 2 would handle the matter and how this would assist him and the management of the leisure group.*

2. *Write brief notes on how, using PRINCE 2, he should approach the control of the project for his own purposes and that of senior management.*

3. *Quality is another item to which your colleague has given little thought. He has imagined going round personally to check "everything is all right" after each sub-contractor finishes. Explain how he might approach the whole quality question, from defining it to checking its presence.*

Marking Scheme for the Example Practitioner Question

Question 1 Reference	Topic	Possible Marks
P1	Project Plan	2
P2	– Purpose	2
P3	– When	2
P4	– Description	2
P5	– Breakdown into Stages	2
S1	Stage Plans	3
S2	– When	2
S3	– Description	2
S4	– Purpose	2
T1	Team Plans	2
T2	– By whom	2
T3	– Description/Link to Work Packages	2
E1	Exception Plans	2
PB1	Product Based Planning	3
PB2	– PBS	2
PB3	– Description	3
PB4	– Product Descriptions	2
PB5	– Description	3
PB5	– Product Flow Diagram	2
PB6	– Description	3
PL	Planning (PL) Process	2
T	Tolerance (1 mark for naming; 2 marks for explanation)	3

Extras

Question 2 Reference	Topic	Possible Marks
1	Controlled Start, Progress and Close	2
2	Design (1 mark) & Appoint (1 mark) Project Management Team	2
3	Project Mandate (1 mark) into Project Brief (1 mark)	2
4	Project Board commitment (1 mark) in IP (or DP2) (1 mark)	2
5	Project Quality Plan (1 mark for name; 1 mark for when created)	2
6	Project Initiation Document (1 mark for name; 1 mark for purpose)	2
7	Project Plan (1 mark for name; 1 for explanation)	2
8	Stages (1 mark for name; 1 mark for concept explanation)	2
9	Business Case (1 mark for name; 1 mark for regular review)	2

Question 2 Reference	Topic	Possible Marks
10	Risks (1 mark for name; 2 marks for continuous assessment)	3
11	Change Control (1 mark for mention; 2 marks for explanation - eg issues (CS3/4))	3
12	Work Package Authorisations (1 mark) Managing Product Delivery (1 mark)	3
13	End Stage Assessments (1 mark for name; 2 marks for purpose)	3
14	– Review current stage (1 mark); Project Plan, Business Case, Risks, Next Plan (1 mark)	2
15	Tolerance (1 mark for name; 1 mark for explanation)	3
16	Exception Procedure (1 mark for name; 1 mark for details)	2
17	Checkpoint Reports (1 mark for name; 1 mark for MP2/CS2 link)	2
18	Highlight Reports (1 mark for name; 1 mark for explanation)	2
19	Management by Exception	2
20	Configuration Management (1 mark for name; 1 mark for explanation)	2
21	Project Closure (1 mark for name; 1 mark for what it does)	2
22	Regular Stage Reviews (1 mark for general mention; 1 mark for CS5)	2
23	Use of Quality Reviews (1 mark); (1 mark for Quality Log)	2

Extras

Question 3 Reference	Topic	Possible Marks
1	Establishing Quality Expectations (2 marks for name; 2 marks for when done)	4
2	Quality Management System	2
3	The role of Quality Assurance	1
4	Project Approach (1 mark for name; 1 mark for when)	2
5	Project Quality Plan (1 mark for name; 1 mark for when; 2 marks for content)	4
6	Stage Quality Plan (1 mark); id Quality Reviewers (2 marks); Assurance (1 mark)	4
7	Product Descriptions (2 marks); Quality Criteria (2 marks); User involvement (1 mark)	5
8	Work Package Authorisations (name 1 mark; PM/TM 1 mark; Quality Reqts 1 mark)	4

Question 3 Reference	Topic	Possible Marks
9	Quality Log (1 mark for name; 2 marks for purpose)	3
10	Use of Quality Reviews	3
11	– Quality Review description	3
12	Quality File (1 mark for name; 1 mark for content/purpose)	2
13	Project Assurance roles (1 mark for name; 2 marks for purpose)	3
14	Checkpoints (1 mark); Highlight Reports (1 mark)	2
15	Recording quality problems on Project Issues	2
16	Use of Configuration Management (2 marks); control & protect Products (2 marks)	4
17	Change Control/Project Issues	2

Extras

The examiner may choose to award additional marks for relevant topics not mentioned in the marking scheme - in theory the number of marks which may be awarded under this category are unrestricted but in practise it is not easy to earn the bonus!

Index compiled by Terry Halliday,
INDEXING SPECIALISTS